Starbiker

Jeremy Strong
Illustrated by Jim Ranson

A & C Black · London

The Crackers Series

The Custard Kid	Terry Deary
Calamity Kate	Terry Deary
Trouble with Animals	Jeremy Strong
The Lambton Worm	Terry Deary
Lightning Lucy	Jeremy Strong
Fatbag	Jeremy Strong
The Wishing Well Ghost	Terry Deary
The Woff	Jeremy Strong
Money doesn't grow on Trees	Jeremy Strong
Eating Ice-cream with a Werewolf	Phyllis Green
Fox on the Roof	Jeremy Strong
Windmill of Nowhere	Terry Deary
Lightning Lucy Strikes Again	Jeremy Strong
Starbiker	Jeremy Strong

Published by A & C Black (Publishers) Limited
35 Bedford Row, London WC1R 4JH

First published 1986

Strong, Jeremy
Starbiker. —— (The Crackers series)
I. Title II. Ranson, Jim III. Series
823'.914[J] PZ7
ISBN 0-7136-2782-4

ISBN 0-7136-2782-4

Filmset by August Filmsetting, Haydock, St. Helens
Printed in Great Britain by R. J. Acford Ltd, Chichester.

1

Death of a bike

'Hey! Here comes the world's fastest bicycle!' yelled Steve from the top of the mound. 'Watch out everybody, Danny's come to burn us up.'

The riders stopped and gazed down at the small boy who was struggling to push his bike up the field towards them. They sat back on their saddles and laughed. Steve tipped up his flashy red helmet. 'Is it a bird? Is it a plane? Is it superbike?' 'No!' cried Paul. 'It's a mistake!'

By this time Danny had reached the mound, panting from his struggle. He smiled at the other boys, gathered round on their BMXs.

'What's that, Maggots?' demanded Paul, pointing at Danny's bike. Danny stiffened. He hated his nickname, and it was all because of his surname, Taggart. He hated people to think that he was thin and pale and wriggly, like a maggot. And he hated his bike.

Danny looked up at Paul and shrugged as if he didn't care. 'It's my bike.'

Paul started to splutter. 'That's not a bike. That's a junk heap on two wheels. I reckon that was built by stone-age man.' The boys laughed again and Steve pulled his front wheel up, spinning, and gave a yell.

'Yee-hah!' He zipped off, pedals whizzing round like a turbo egg-whisk. The others peeled off after him, racing down off the mound and away over the rutted path they used as a track.

Danny watched them disappear in a glitter of chrome. He looked down at his bike ruefully. It was a bit old. The paint was rusty. The saddle was squeezed and squashed, as if an elephant had been asleep on it for the last twenty years. The tyres were old and black. Nobody had black tyres anymore! They had red, or blue or yellow ones. Yellow was amazing, but you could only get black for his type of bike – the stone-age type.

He climbed onto the saddle and tried to do a wheelie like Steve. The bike reared up. Danny wobbled back, waggling his front wheel desperately. Then the whole muddle crashed sideways into the bushes. Danny thrashed about a bit and struggled out, scratched and stung by some nettles.

It was no good. His bike wasn't balanced like the BMXs. They were specially built for that sort of trick. Danny scratched his stings and gazed down the hill in the direction the pack had gone. Oh well, at least his bike could go just as fast – downhill. He scrambled back on the bike and set off after them.

He found the others outside the park, staring over the railings.

'I can't see Creakyboots anywhere,' murmured

Pete. 'I reckon it's safe to go in. Even if he sees us, we can ride off.'

'You said that last time, and look what happened. He came round and spoke to my Dad and I wasn't allowed to ride my bike for a week.' Steve glared at Pete.

'Well it's stupid. Why can't we ride in the park? Look at it. It's practically empty. What harm can we do? It's got much better tracks than up by the mound.'

Steve still hung back. 'I don't trust that park-keeper. Creakyboots is always nosing around. I reckon he's probably a Russian spy.'

The boys began to laugh, but Danny looked at Steven seriously. 'Is he really a Russian spy?'

Steven groaned out loud and the others laughed even more. Paul patted Danny on the back like a dog. 'Of course he is. Didn't you know? This park is a secret missile base. Those benches are really radar scanners and all the missiles are hidden in the trees.

The other boys were trying hard not to laugh, but David started spluttering and then everybody broke down into giggles. Danny watched with a half smile, wondering what they were on about.

'Come on,' cried Steve, and he led the way into the park.

Danny followed, some way behind. There were little paths all over the park that were ideal. The

BMX boys raced round, leaping and skidding and doing all their favourite tricks. Danny joined in as best he could. He pedalled furiously and flung his bike round the corners like a grand prix racer, trying to do all the endos and aerials the others did.

'Oi!' There was a shout from behind and over a crest of grass a large flying figure appeared, crouched low over the bars of a racing bike.

'Yike!' squealed Steve. 'It's Creakyboots, and he's on a bike – scram!' He stood hard on the pedals and went scooting off with the other three BMXs close behind. The park-keeper waved a fist in the air but it made him wobble so much he hurriedly grabbed the handlebars once more.

'Hey, come back! You know you're not supposed to ride round here. Just you wait.' Then he saw Danny, trying to creep behind the climbing frame.

'You little monster! I'll teach you a lesson . . .'

Danny scrambled onto the saddle and darted round the side of the climbing frame. The park-keeper was travelling so fast he overshot Danny by several metres and had to skid to a halt, ploughing up his own precious grass. Creakyboots jerked round and came back after Danny, who was twisting and turning like a rabbit with the hounds after it. It was quite clear what was going to happen next.

There was a hideous crunch, two sharp yells, a big thud, a little thud, another yell plus a noise like all the air being let out of an elephant, several little tinkles, a long scrape and then silence.

At the bottom of the pile was the racing bike, it's front wheel slowly spinning round. On top of that was the park-keeper. His hat had somehow got stuck onto his left foot. On top of Creakyboots sat Danny, clasping his leg to his chest and trying to stop the bleeding from a long cut down one shin. Resting upside down against Danny's back was what was left of his bike. The rear wheel was buckled and the mudguard had fallen off. The handlebars were twisted round and one of the pedals had been bent under so much pressure that it had snapped off and stabbed itself into the grass.

Creakyboots pulled himself out of the mess. He yanked his bicycle upright and eyed it gingerly. 'Look at that,' he muttered, kicking a damaged wheel. Danny rocked back and forth, hugging his leg. 'Brand new and all,' went on the park-keeper. He glanced at Danny's wreck and grunted. 'Not much left of yours, is there, you young hooligan. Maybe that will teach you.'

'I wasn't doing any harm,' murmured Danny.

'Wasn't doing any harm! Wasn't doing any harm!' echoed the park-keeper.

'Well I wasn't,' said Danny.

'You ought to be locked up,' said Creakyboots stiffly. 'Here, what have you done to your leg?'

'Not much.'

'Doesn't look like not much to me. Show me.'

Creakyboots crouched down and straightened Danny's leg out. 'It's not a deep cut. I don't think you'll bleed to death this week. Come on. You'd better come over to my shed and we'll get you patched up.' He helped Danny to his feet and they began to walk over to the park-keeper's shed. Danny looked back at the bikes.

'What about my bike?' he asked.

'You want me to patch that up as well?' Creakyboots almost laughed at the idea, which took Danny by surprise.

'No, I mean, suppose somebody steals it?'

That really did make the keeper laugh. 'I don't think anyone will steal your bike. In fact you'll probably have to pay somebody just to take it away for scrap. Come on. Let's get that leg clean.'

Ten minutes later Danny left the shed with his leg

covered in bandage. Creakyboots wasn't very good at first aid and the leg looked as if it had escaped from an Egyptian mummy. Danny collected his bike, but it was impossible to ride. When he got to the park gates he found Steve and the BMX gang there, waiting to see what awful things had happened to Danny.

'Here he comes,' said Paul, and he shouted out. 'What happened Maggots? What did he do to you?' All eyes boggled as Danny wheeled his wreck through the gate.

'We crashed,' said Danny simply.

'Crashed? Oh wow! What happened?'

'Well, my bike fell to bits and his wheel got all buckled.'

The boys looked at each other and drew in their breath sharply. Steve's jaw dropped another five centimetres.

'You bust old Creakyboots' bike?' Danny nodded. 'What did he do?'

'Took me to his shed.' The boys stared. It was getting worse and worse. They couldn't imagine how Danny had even managed to get out alive.

'Go on! Go on! What did he do then?' demanded David.

Danny looked down at the pavement. 'He bandaged my leg.'

'Bandaged your leg?' David screwed up his face in disbelief.

'Yes.'

There was a short silence while the boys tried to get to grips with this startling piece of information. Then Steven croaked 'What did you say?'

Danny shrugged. 'Thank you, of course. I'm going home now. See you.' And he went trudging down the road, trailing bits of bike.

2

The Raffle

Mr and Mrs Taggart were not very impressed when they saw Danny's bike. He left it in a heap beside the garden shed and Dad thought the neighbours had been throwing rubbish over the wall. 'Sandra managed to ride that bike for years without breaking anything,' Mr Taggart pointed out. Sandra was Danny's thirteen year old sister.

'It wasn't my fault. Anyway, we've had that bike for ages and it's old and rusty and a girl's bike. The other boys laugh at me when I ride it.'

'I can't help that. I can't afford to buy you another bike so unless you manage to repair this you haven't got one at all.'

Danny moaned as he stared at the rusty pile. 'Couldn't I have a BMX like the others?' Mr Taggart looked sideways at his son.

'Do you know how much a BMX is?' he asked. Danny shook his head. 'I'll tell you.They're too much, that's how much they are.' And he walked off.

Danny sat down on a log. It was quite true. He knew BMXs were expensive and he knew they couldn't afford it. Mrs Taggart came out and looked at him.

'Sorry about the bike, Danny,' she said. 'You know how it is, with your Dad not working and everything . . .'

'Yeah, I know.' Mrs Taggart shrugged and went back indoors.

Danny stayed put and gazed round at nothing in particular, thinking. What would it be like if they became millionaires overnight? Dad could have a Rolls Royce, and he could have a Rolls Royce BMX and Mum could have a Rolls Royce washing machine and Sandra could have . . . What would Sandra want? All she seemed to do these days was wash her hair and stick it in curlers. Maybe there was a Rolls Royce hair drier? He wandered indoors to see if tea was ready.

Sandra was standing in front of the hall mirror, making up her eyes with green shadow. Danny stood beside her and looked over her shoulder. Sandra gazed at her brother's reflection. 'Look at that,' she muttered. 'Beauty and the Beast.'

Danny grinned. 'Oh, I don't know. You're not so bad really.'

'I meant you Danny! You're the beast, not me,

and if you go making rude comments about me I won't give you what I picked up in the new superstore today.' Sandra put down her comb and pulled out an envelope.

'What's in it?' asked Danny, trying to grab the envelope from Sandra's waving hands.

'Tell me I'm gorgeous,' said Sandra.

'You're gorgeous. Oh, come on!'

'Say I'm wonderful, beautiful, amazing and out of this world.'

'You're out of this world all right. If you put on any more make-up you'll look like a Martian.' Sandra narrowed her eyes and started to put the envelope away. 'But you are beautiful,' Danny added hastily, and she handed the paper over.

Danny opened it up and pulled out a slip. It was a ticket for a grand raffle. The first prize was a dish-washer. Ugh. The second prize was a tumble-drier. Third prize was a Starstriker BMX with full racing kit. Fourth prize was WHAT!! Who cared what the fourth prize was? It was the third prize that Danny was going for. He grabbed Sandra and hugged her and planted huge kisses on both her cheeks.

'Thanks Sandra! Hey Mum! Look at this, look!'

Mum smiled and kept her thoughts to herself. She had been to hundreds of raffles and only once won a prize – a tube of shaving cream. As Mrs Taggart had pointed out, if she'd had a beard and moustache it might have been useful. As it was she gave it to Mr Taggart. The chances of Danny winning any prize was probably one in a million.

Danny couldn't sit still during tea. He kept looking at his ticket and trying to imagine what a Starstriker BMX was like. 'I've never heard of that make, have you, Mum? What do you think they mean by "full kit"?'

'I don't know. What do you normally wear for a BMX?' Danny explained that the children didn't usually have kits. That came extra and he had never seen a proper kit.

'There'll be a helmet,' he went on, 'and trousers with padded knees, and gloves, and a jacket with padded elbows . . .'

'What are they padded for?' Mum asked.

'In case you fall off, of course.'

'In case you fall off? It sounds very dangerous.'

'People are always falling off BMXs,' Danny said proudly.

'Why? Can't they ride properly?'

'Yes! Of course they can, but, well, they keep falling off.'

'Sounds daft to me.'

'But you're meant to fall off,' Danny shouted.

Mum opened her eyes so wide they almost tumbled out of her face. 'Are you telling me that you wanted us to spend a fortune on a bike so that you could fall off it?'

There was a long silence while Danny cleared his head of all the questions that were buzzing round inside like angry wasps. At last he got himself together and told his mother about all the tricks you could do on a BMX, and that the clothing was for protection, just in case.

Mrs Taggart still thought the whole thing sounded crazy, but she told Danny she hoped he won the bike anyway, and since the raffle was the next day he wouldn't have long to wait. Danny did not get much sleep that night. He spent most of his time riding dream BMXs round the park. First of all he did the most amazing aerials that had Steve and Paul and the other boys falling off their saddles in surprise. Then Creakyboots came along and tried to catch him, but Danny was so nimble and skilful that the park-keeper just stood there and clapped.

'Go to sleep,' said Mr Taggart, when he poked his head round the bedroom door at half past ten. Danny sighed and turned to the wall. Even so, he didn't get to sleep until he had heard the old clock on the biscuit factory strike twelve.

The next day came at last. The raffle was going to take place in the afternoon. Danny spent the entire morning walking round and round, looking at his watch to see what the time was. Mum sliced up some potatoes for lunch and watched him.

'What will you do if you don't win the bike?' she asked.

'What? You mean if I win the dish-washer or tumble-drier?'

'No! Of course not. Suppose you win nothing?' For a moment Danny stared at his mother. That was a daft idea.

'There's no point in having a ticket if you don't win anything,' he said.

'But it is the luck of the draw,' Mrs Taggart continued. 'There'll be thousands of tickets and only a few prizes.' She went on quietly slicing the potatoes while Danny walked round and round.

Sandra came in and said she would go to the raffle with Danny. After all, he might need some help carrying home his prizes.

'I shall ride it home,' Danny insisted.

'Suppose it's the dish-washer? You can't ride that.' Danny glared at his sister and carried on wearing out the carpet.

Lunch came and went too slowly. As soon as it was over the pair of them set off for the new supermarket where the raffle was being held. It was a publicity stunt to launch the new store and when they arrived the celebrity guest was already there. She was a well-known TV star, stunningly beautiful and elegant.

'Oh I wish I looked like that,' Sandra murmured dreamily.

'So would Dad,' grinned Danny.

The star may have looked wonderful, but sadly her voice sounded like empty tin cans going round a giant food mixer. 'It's absolutely *lovely* to be here, and I'm reely reely *honoured* and *delighted*. You're all so *lovely* and this is a *fantastic* shop, isn't it? What a *super* raffle, with lots of *gorgeous* prizes. There's a dish-washer and a tumble-drier and um, er, . . .'

Here the shop manager leaned over and whispered into her ear. 'Ooh, don't nibble my ear, you naughty man! The third prize is an amazing BMX.' She turned to the manager. 'What's a BMX?' she hissed. 'Oh! A bike! Isn't that nice! Now I'm going to put my hand in the box and pull out the first ticket . . .'

'Quick, what's your number?' asked Sandra.

Danny whipped out his ticket and glanced at it: 67525. For a terrible moment he wondered if that meant there were at least sixty-seven thousand five hundred and twenty five tickets.

'The first prize is 3019. 3019.' There was a yell from the middle of the crowd and a lady jumped up and down excitedly.

'Well that's the dish-washer gone, but there are

still lots more *amazing* prizes, all donated by this *wonderful* store. The second ticket is coming out now, isn't this *exciting* and it's 13008.'

This time a man near the front went quietly forward. He didn't really want a tumble-drier and had been hoping for the case of whisky. But he cheered up when the TV star gave him a kiss on the cheek and shook his hand.

Danny took a deep breath and closed his eyes, memorising his number – 67525. He kept telling himself that he wouldn't draw another breath until the number was announced, but he could hardly bear to listen. So many thousands of people and so many thousands of tickets. It was impossible.

'And now the third ticket is coming out and it's number 67525!'

The number slammed through Danny's brain like an enormous hammer. He felt Sandra grip his arm in wild delight. He breathed out at last and fainted from the strain. He sank gently into a crumpled heap on the pavement.

3

Starstriker

Danny lay like a crumpled white bedsheet on the concrete. Sandra bent over him, anxiously tugging at one arm. 'Danny! Stop mucking about – you've won! Wake up!'

The famous TV star was calling out the winning number once more, and getting cross about it. 'Is the winner here? The number is 67525 and what a *marvellous* prize it is – a de-luxe, supersonic, remote controlled steam iron with special . . . what?' The shop manager was nudging her again. 'Oops, sorry, silly me! Of course it's the MXB with lots of wonderful extras! There's a saddle and two wheels and um, handlebars and er – *will nobody claim this prize*?' The star screeched.

At the back of the crowd a young man bent over Danny. 'I'm a doctor,' he announced.

'Please wake him up,' pleaded Sandra. The doctor gazed at Danny.

'He's fainted,' he said.

'For the very last time,' shrieked the TV star. 'The winner of the BXM full colour steam iron is ticket number 67525.'

The doctor lifted Danny in his arms. 'We must get out of this crowd, then he'll be okay,' he said, and he began to back out of the crowd. 'It's the heat that was too much for him.'

Sandra danced up and down beside the tall doctor. 'It's nothing to do with the heat. Danny's won the third prize and it was the shock. Look, here's the ticket, and if he doesn't claim the prize now they'll draw another ticket and oh, it's awful, I don't know . . . ' And Sandra burst into tears.

'Time's up!' shouted the TV star. 'I'm going to draw another ticket.'

The doctor glanced at sobbing Sandra, suddenly made sense of everything and went charging through the crowd, knocking people aside like skittles. 'The winner's here!' he yelled. 'Stop the draw! The winner's here!'

The TV star glared back at the strange rhinoceros thundering towards her. 'Well it took you long enough,' she snapped. 'Come here and collect your prize, but I must say you look rather big to go around playing on a bicycle.' The crowd began to laugh, but the doctor lifted Danny up and explained everything. The manager immediately had Danny taken inside the store and settled on a chair. The colour drifted back to his cheeks and gradually he regained consciousness.

'Feel better now?' enquired the manager.

Danny gazed round, trying to work out where he was. All at once he remembered the raffle.

'It's gone! My ticket!' He grasped Sandra and

jumped up, wildly searching his pockets. The doctor calmed Danny down and at the same time the third prize was wheeled forward. It was covered in flat cardboard and all Danny could see were the bottoms of the wheels and the handlebars and saddle sticking out of the top.

One of the shop assistants brought out a smaller parcel. 'That's the gear that goes with it,' said the manager. 'Congratulations. I hope you like your new BMX.'

Danny held the handlebars and looked at his prize. He could hardly believe any of it, but there it was, actually in his own hands, with the doctor and his sister both grinning at him like monkeys in a banana tree.

'Come on,' said Sandra, 'Let's get home and have a look. Thank very much for your help,' she said to the doctor. 'I'm sorry I was rude to you.' The doctor smiled as if it didn't matter and watched them as they wheeled the bike out through a side door.

All the way home, practically running, Danny and Sandra went over the events of the raffle again and again. Now it was over they could laugh about it.

Mr and Mrs Taggart were amazed when they saw Danny coming down the road with his prize, but all the amazement became wonder when Danny stripped the cardboard away from the bike to reveal its glory.

The BMX was a dazzling silver all over, a silver that shimmered and glittered with all the colours of the rainbow. The saddle, tyres and grips were bright blue. Along the crossbar in metallic lettering was the word STARSTRIKER, and there were shooting stars of different sizes and colours all down both sides of the frame.

Danny grinned and ran his hands over the frame. He was surprised to discover that each star had a tiny bulge to it. When he looked more closely he could see that the centre of each star was slightly raised. It didn't seem to affect the paintwork so it must have been manufactured like that on purpose.

'You lucky devil,' smiled Mum.

'I reckon we should have got tickets for that raffle,' said Dad. 'We might have been lucky too. Just look at it. I've never seen a bike as smart as that.'

'You haven't looked in the other parcel yet, Danny,' said Sandra.

Being so overcome with the BMX, Danny had forgotten about all the gear. He tore off the brown paper and pulled out a silver helmet, silver trousers and silver jacket. Like the bike, they flashed every colour in the sunlight.

'Wow!' breathed Danny, laying them carefully on the grass. Sandra staggered back, shielding her eyes.

'Help, I've gone blind from the glare. It's all too much for me.'

'Don't be daft,' laughed Dad. 'But I've got to admit that's quite a bike and quite a suit. Get the gear on! Let's have a look!'

The rest of the family were almost as excited as Danny. He rushed inside and came out two minutes later transformed. The suit fitted perfectly. The helmet glistened on his head. Danny climbed onto the BMX and grinned at his family.

'All right,' said mum, 'you great big show-off!'

'Yeeeee-*hah*!' Danny yelled and tore away down the road.

The other boys were up by the mound. Paul watched the glittering bike as it made its way nearer. 'Who's that?'

'I don't know,' grunted Steve. 'Who do you think I am? X-ray man? I can't see through all that get-up.

'Looks very flashy,' murmured Pete.

Danny rode up and stopped. He pulled off the helmet and scratched his hair where it itched from wearing the crash-hat.

'Hey! It's Maggots! Where did you get that?'

'I won it in the Superstore raffle,' Danny said. Pete read the writing on the frame.

'Starstriker. I've never heard of that make, have you?' The others shook their heads.

'Probably some crummy cheap make,' jeered Paul.

'It's not crummy!' yelled Danny. 'It can beat you lot any day, so there!'

'Oh yeah? I reckon your BMX will fall to bits at the first jump just like your old girl's bike.'

'Right,' said Danny. 'Come on. Line up and I'll race you.'

'You're on. Down to that tree, back up over the mound, through the dip and back to the tree. Okay?'

Danny pulled his helmet on and tightened the strap. He raised one pedal ready for push off and crouched over the handlebars. '3, 2, 1, Go!' screamed Dave, and the bikes poured away down the hill to the tree. Danny was up near the front, pedals whizzing round. Past the tree he went, too wide, and lost time doing an unnecessary skid. He trailed up the hill panting furiously, with the other bikes a little ahead. Then over the mound with both wheels off the ground. Danny landed badly, taking all the shock in his back rather than his legs. He charged through the dip and went zooming back down to the tree.

The gang was already waiting for him, hands on hips and smiling and panting at the same time. 'See,' said Steve. 'Told you. That bike's crummy. Come on you lot, let's go.' He turned away and they went slowly down the hill.

Danny stood astride his bike getting back his breath. There were hot tears waiting in his eyes but he wouldn't let them trickle out. He punched his hands together miserably. It wasn't fair. They were all at least three years older and he'd never even ridden a BMX before.

Somebody spoke, making him jump. 'Do you want to try again?'

'What?' Danny wheeled round but couldn't see anybody.

'Do you want to try again?' The voice was quiet and firm.

'Who are you?' Danny demanded.

'Starstriker.'

'Starstriker? My bike?' Danny looked at his BMX. No, that wasn't possible. 'You can't be,' said Danny, beginning to feel rather stupid, talking to thin air.

'Oh? Why not?'

Danny shrugged. 'Bikes don't talk!' He wrinkled his nose.

'Oh. I'll shut-up then. Goodbye.'

There was a silence, while Danny thought. At length he said, 'There's no need to go all sulky on me. Can you really speak?'

'Of course. Can't you see?' And now that Danny looked, he could see. The bike flickered with tiny lights as it spoke, and so did the helmet. All those knobbly stars were little lights and now that he was getting used to it, Danny realised that the voice was coming from within the helmet itself.

'So,' said Starstriker. 'Do you want to try again? All you need is a bit of experience. I can soon show you how to ride properly, and when that's done I can show you what else I can do.'

'You mean you can do more than talk?'

'Of course. Let's go back to that rather muddy mound and I'll show you everything.'

Danny got onto the saddle and pedalled up to the mound. 'This is fantastic,' he murmured. 'Nobody will ever believe me.'

Starstriker almost sighed. 'Yes, I'm afraid people can be like that at times. Never mind, we'll make the best of it. Here we are. Urrgh, it is rather messy up here, isn't it? You will make sure to give me a bath when we get home, won't you?'

Danny laughed. 'Starstriker, if you are as amazing as I think I'll give you a hot water bottle if you really want one. Now let's go!'

4

Starstruck!

With the daylight drifting towards evening, Danny practised and practised. His big silver helmet was strapped tightly across his jaw, the mysterious stars on it twinkling in the gloom as Starstriker guided Danny in every move he made.

'You're making your body lean over too far ... straighten up ... don't waggle the bike between your legs like that, it wastes energy ... front brake a touch before the rear on this corner ... legs straight as you leap ...'

At last they halted and Danny pulled the helmet off. He wiped the sweat from his smudged face and grinned. He was exhausted and his legs felt like lumps of lead from the hard pedalling, but inside he felt fantastic – like a huge, laughing giant. He sat down against a tree trunk with the helmet in his lap and the bike propped up on its stand.

'Wow! I can really ride like a star now!'

'You'll do for the time being,' answered Starstriker. Danny's jaw dropped.

'But I could easily beat the other boys now. You wait and see.'

'I don't want to wait and see. Of course you could beat the older boys. I'm not talking about being better than them. I mean being even better than you are now, learning to take corners more finely, jump higher and land better. You will always be improving.'

Danny listened and dug his fingers into the grass, pulling out bits of weed to throw away. 'I suppose so,' he muttered. Starstriker's frame glittered.

'I haven't shown you what *I* can do yet.'

'How do you mean?' asked Danny.

The helmet twinkled. 'Let's go round once more.'

'Oh no! I don't think I've got the energy,' moaned Danny.

'I have,' said Starstriker. 'Get on.'

Danny pulled on the helmet and set off. As they went over the rough course he began to wonder if he was dreaming. He didn't seem to be in control of the BMX at all. They shot round the course at fantastic speed, yet he hardly felt a bump. All at once the mound loomed up in front like a huge, escaped whale.

'Slow down Starstriker! We can't jump thaaaagh!!' The bike powered into the dark air, flying over the mound in a glittering silent arc. Halfway over, the BMX twisted round in a double spin. Danny closed his eyes in terror, then the ground flashed up, but there was hardly a jolt as the bike landed and immediately slewed round sharply to take the hill, stretching up before them.

Danny's feet barely touched the pedals, but

Starstriker thundered up the steep slope and didn't stop until they reached the crest. Danny gazed back in a trance.

'Did I do all that?' he whispered.

'No. I did.'

'But how did you do that jump?'

'Let's say I've got one or two extras inside my frame that other bikes haven't even heard of.'

Danny tipped his helmet up and stuck both hands on his hips.

'Where do you come from?' he demanded.

'You won me in a raffle.'

'Oh come on! You know what I mean.'

There was a long silence until at last the little stars on the BMX twinkled and Starstriker spoke. 'I think it must be time to get home and have tea. It seems to be getting dark.'

Realising that he wasn't going to get a reply, Danny got on the bike and pedalled slowly down the hill and onto the street. Steve and Paul were cruising round aimlessly. Danny smiled.

'Starstriker?'

'Hmmm?'

'You know your hidden extras? Do you think we could do just one jump as we go past Steve and Paul? Just to show them?'

'You mean to show off?'

Danny reddened. 'I suppose so,' he muttered. There was a sigh from Starstriker.

'Just when I was enjoying a peaceful ride home. All right, one jump coming up, full Thunderthrust.'

Danny immediately felt the bike quicken beneath him, and he crouched lower over the bars. The silver frame sparkled and they headed straight for the two older boys.

'Wey-hey!' cried Paul. 'here comes Maggots on his penny-farthing!'

Steve watched the approaching bike. 'He's got quite a speed up. He's coming straight at us.' There was rising panic in his voice and he yelled out. 'Hey, watch it Maggots! Put your brakes . . .' His voice died in his throat as Danny and Starstriker suddenly climbed into the air. Paul and Steve automatically threw themselves to the ground and covered their heads. 'The idiot's going to squash us!' screamed Steve, bracing himself for the crunch.

'Yeee-hah!' yelled Danny as the bike sailed way over the two boys and landed far beyond them, only to disappear round the corner with a twinkle of sparkling stars.

Paul and Steve slowly sat up. 'Did you see that?' asked Steve huskily. 'I don't believe it. Was that a bike or a UFO?'

Paul shook his head. 'It's not possible.'

Steve got to his feet. 'I'm going home. I've had enough of Maggots and his bikes. See you tomorrow.'

When Danny went indoors Mum and Dad and Sandra were sitting at table with empty plates. They had been finished for five minutes and Mrs Taggart wasn't too pleased with Danny's late arrival.

'Hurry up and sit down. Your food is cold, I'm sure.' said Mrs Taggart. Danny started to eat.

'You know what, Mum?' he began.

'Yes, I do know what. Don't talk with your mouth full.'

'But Mum, Starstriker can talk.'

'And you shouldn't,' repeated Mum. 'Not with your mouth full.'

'He's got the table manners of a Komodo dragon,' Sandra said.

Everyone turned and looked at her. 'A what?'

'A Komodo dragon. I saw one on telly last week. They live on an island and they grab their prey and tear it up with their jaws. Then they stick their front legs in – they've got very sharp claws you see – and they sort of go urraurraurra . . .' Sandra waved her sharp front claws about. Mum sat back a bit.

'Charming,' she murmured. Sandra looked at her brother.

'Anyway, he's like one of those.'

'Urraurraurra!' growled Danny, until Dad told him off smartly.

Danny remembered the bike and started once more. 'My BMX can talk,' he announced.

'Oh, that's nice,' said Mum, quite disbelievingly.

'He can! Starstriker can talk and he tells me what to do and how to take corners and everything, and then he goes on Thunderthrust and jumps, pyowwwwww!'

'Don't wave your fork in the air like that!' snapped Mum.

Danny looked at his mother and father and sister. 'You don't believe me, do you? You think I'm making it all up.'

Sandra started to laugh. 'Really Danny, don't you think you're getting a bit old for that sort of make-believe?'

Danny banged the table angrily with one fist, making the jam pot jump up and fall over. He ran to the hall and grabbed his helmet. 'Just listen,' he shouted, putting the helmet on the table in front of everybody. 'Starstriker!'

The crash-hat shone silver in the lamplight. 'Starstriker?' There was quiet. Danny chewed his lip. The others looked at each other and Sandra tapped her head as if to say her brother was going mad. 'Starstriker?' Danny glanced up frantically, a tear in one eye.

Mr Taggart put a hand on his shoulder. 'Come on Danny. I think you've got a bit over-excited with everything that's happened today. How about some sleep?'

'But he can talk!' cried Danny, grabbing the helmet and knocking on it in sheer desperation. 'Starstriker! Please talk to me!' Mrs Taggart was now looking very worried and she moved to the telephone to call a doctor.

'Starstriker!'

The helmet suddenly twinkled and a tired voice spoke. 'What now? I was having a peaceful doze and somebody has to come and shout at me. Haven't I done enough today?'

The telephoned dangled silently from Mum's hand. Dad crashed back into an armchair, while Danny swept the helmet up and hugged it. 'See – I said he can talk, and he can!'

'He can talk,' choked Mum.

'He can talk,' said Dad, his lips moving almost silently.

Sandra stood up. 'It's a tape recording,' she declared. 'I've seen it done on telly.'

'Oh shut-up,' said Danny and Mum and Dad together.

Starstriker yawned. 'That is a very good suggestion, then maybe I can get some sleep. Please don't knock on my helmet again Danny, it gives me a headache. Where do you sleep?'

'Me? I've got a bedroom upstairs.'

The crash-hat sparkled. 'Good. That will do nicely. Goodnight.'

The Taggarts looked at one another in puzzlement. Mum was just about to pinch herself to see if she was dreaming, when there came a weird rumbling sound from beyond the door. Dad climbed out of his chair and went through to the hall. 'If that's Snapper jumping on the settee again I'll wring his – oh no! I don't believe it.'

The others rushed out just in time to see Starstriker disappearing up the stairs, all by himself, bumping clumsily over the steps. At the top the bike stopped. 'Which is your room?' demanded the BMX.

Before Danny could answer, Mr Taggart had pointed downstairs and said very sternly, 'you stay down here in the hall. You can sleep by the door. I am not having talking bicycles in the bedroom.'

Starstriker bounced stiffly back down the stairs and parked himself near the front door. The silver frame sparkled. 'Come to think of it, I shall prefer it down here. People can be so unpleasant, can't they Danny?' And before anybody could think of a reply, Starstriker was sound asleep.

5

Starstriker goes to school

It took Mr and Mrs Taggart a little time to get used to the idea of a talking bicycle. It must have seemed rather silly to have conversations with a crash helmet, even if it did have shooting stars that shone.

One morning Mrs Taggart came in from the garden looking for Danny. She wandered into the front room, thinking out loud.

'I wonder where he is?'

'Upstairs in his bedroom,' said the helmet on the table. Mrs Taggart yelped and dropped the flower-pot she was carrying. There was a crash and bits of pot shot across the carpet. Mrs Taggart bent down and began to scoop up the shattered fragments, shaking her head.

'It's not right, not right at all – talking helmets and flying bicycles . . .'

'Quite frankly,' murmured Starstriker, 'it seems very right to me. I don't know how you managed before with all those silent machines.'

Mrs Taggart waved her dustpan at the helmet. 'It was a lot easier to understand, that's what. And I can tell you it was very nice simply riding along without the blooming bicycle interrupting you all the time. Very peaceful it was.'

The helmet sighed. 'Danny's stopped playing. He's coming downstairs. I think you were going to ask him something.'

Mrs Taggart got up from the floor. 'Oh yes, about the bread.' She scowled and looked back at the crash-hat. 'How did you know all that?'

'All what?'

'That Danny was in his bedroom, then that he was coming downstairs *and* you knew I wanted to ask him something.'

'Perhaps I'm just very clever,' said Starstriker. Mrs Taggart rolled her eyes at the large helmet.

'Hmmm – well you've certainly got the biggest head I've ever seen.' And she went to find Danny.

Similar surprises happened at school. People were amazed and baffled by Danny's BMX, but they were also impressed, especially the first time that he brought Starstriker to school. There was a cycle shed at the back of the main building, but Danny stayed on the playground, which wasn't allowed. Children clustered round the glittering machine.

'Are you going to ride it then?'

'Of course I am.'

'You're not allowed to ride in the playground,' said Terry, rather angelically. Danny shrugged, feeling very proud and brave.

One of the girls touched the handlebars. 'Why do you call it Starstriker? You make it sound like a person.' Danny grinned.

'It is a person, sort of.'

The children laughed. Danny looked at their smiling faces. He tightened the strap on his helmet. 'You tell them Starstriker.'

'Tell them what?' The tiny lights sparkled.

'Tell them you're a person.'

'I'm a person,' declared the bike.

The onlookers were listening in stupefied silence. At last Tracy managed to squeak: 'It can talk!'

'Congratulations,' murmured Starstriker. 'You've noticed.'

A thin, small boy pushed forward. 'It can't be a person. People have arms and legs and everything.' Starstriker waggled a wheel.

'My handlebars are arms. As for legs, who wants those silly sticks? Wheels are a great deal faster. Danny, I think it's time we showed this lot what we can do. Let's go.'

Danny grabbed the handlebars and they sped to the far end of the playground. Back they came, twisting and turning with startling precision. Suddenly the bike stopped dead, holding the balance on the spot. All at once the BMX leaped straight into the air, twisting to land in the opposite direction. Starstriker accelerated away at tremendous speed.

'That's full Powerboost,' explained Starstriker quietly.

'I know. Do you think we can take that crowd?' They skidded round to face the fascinated children. Starstriker flashed in the sunlight.

'No problem at all,' The BMX shot forward and zoomed into the air, powering over the children below, to land in a little burst of burning rubber from the tyres.

'Wow!' squealed the crowd, and at that moment one of the teachers walked onto the playground. It was Mrs Shenally.

'That boy!' she yelled. 'Come here!' The crowd hurriedly vanished. Danny pushed back his helmet and pedalled slowly over to his teacher. 'What do you think you're up to?' demanded Mrs Shenally.

'I was showing everyone my new BMX. I won it in a raffle.'

'I don't care if it fell out of a packet of Cornflakes,' cried Mrs Shenally. 'You don't ride on the playground.'

The bike twinkled. 'Who is this rude person?' demanded Starstriker. Mrs Shenally went cross-eyed with shock and gave a giant twitch, as if she had just trodden on a King Cobra.

'Sssh,' whispered Danny. 'It's my teacher, Mrs Shenally.'

'I don't care if she's the Empress of China,' said Starstriker. 'There's no need to make rude remarks about me. Fell out of a packet of Cornflakes. Huh!'

Mrs Shenally had turned as white as spilt milk. She stared at Danny and pointed at the bike, unable to speak. Her mouth moved silently and Danny guessed she was saying something about Starstriker being a talking bicycle. He explained all about the BMX, while Mrs Shenally slowly nodded her head as if she understood, but her face still looked like wallpaper paste.

Danny thought everything was all right, and he began to show Mrs Shenally what Starstriker could do, hopping up and down on one wheel and doing jumps from side to side. Mrs Shenally found her voice at last.

'Stop it! Stop it at once!' she screamed. Starstriker obviously decided he had had enough of this noisy lady and he instantly took off down the playground steps and zipped into the school. 'Come back!' squealed Mrs Shenally, running after Danny and the bike, waving both arms as if she'd been dropped from a plane without a parachute.

As Starstriker careered down the school corridors, it was all Danny could do to keep himself safely on the saddle. 'Stop, Starstriker, please!' he pleaded.

'That creature won't catch us,' declared the bike, and Starstriker skidded round a corner only to come face to face with the Headmaster, Mr Coker.

'Argh!' he gurgled. 'Get off that bicycle at once!'

'Sorry – can't stop!' cried Danny as the BMX hurtled past the astonished man and raced on past the classrooms. Puzzled by all the noise, other teachers stepped into the corridor to see what was going on. Some had their toes run over, other leaped back just in time. One unlucky man was caught by his arm and sent spinning like a gyroscope back into his classroom where he crashed into his cupboard and slumped down into the wastepaper bin.

'I'm beginning to enjoy this,' murmured Stars-

triker brightly, while Danny said little prayers to himself over and over again, wishing the nightmare would stop.

It was then that the BMX discovered the main hall, which had just been set up for a gym period.

'Hold tight Danny!' cried Starstriker, shooting up a plank and wobbling along the balance beam. 'This is what I've been dreaming about all my life! It's paradise!'

Starstriker bounced down a ladder on the other side, zoomed to the end of the hall, shot up to the vaulting box and took it in a flying jump with triple twist.

'Get off that equipment!' yelled Mr Coker, clambering after the bike with as much puffing and panting as a walrus in a marathon.

'Don't worry, Mr Coker,' said the gym master, 'I'll get him!' Timing himself perfectly, the gym master grabbed a rope from the climbing apparatus and launched himself nimbly across the hall in a swooshing arc.

Starstriker spotted the flying enemy just in time, spun on the spot and nipped back onto the balancing beam, while the gym master swung back straight into the headmaster, knocking him from the vaulting box where he had perched to issue his orders. Mr Coker disappeared over the edge and landed with a fatty thud on the thick mat.

Starstriker now looked round for a means of escape, but finding none he simply came to a halt in the middle of the hall. 'There! That was good, wasn't it Danny?' Feeling sick from head to toe, Danny gazed round at all the faces peering at him, staring at him, closing in on him.

'Starstriker,' he groaned. 'I can feel my funeral coming up. At least, it's either my funeral or my breakfast.' A firm hand grasped Danny's arm and he let himself be lifted off the bike. He looked up into Mr Coker's big, red, scowling face.

'I think you have some explaining to do,' said the Headmaster.

Danny sat down on a box and began. He started at the beginning and went right the way through, making a thousand apologies for Starstriker's behaviour as he went.

'But he can't help it, you see. He doesn't understand.'

The BMX thrust a wheel forward.'Oh yes I do understand. That woman was very rude to me out on the playground. I'm quite sure, Mr Coker, that you wouldn't let anybody speak to you like that.'

'I certainly wouldn't,' said Mr Coker gruffly.

'There you are then.'

'But I'm not a bicycle!' cried Mr Coker. 'I'm a human being!'

'I can't help that,' said the bike regretfully. 'We all have our problems, don't we?'

At length, despite Starstriker's very unhelpful interruptions, everything was explained and Danny was quite forgiven for the wondrous things that had happened. The teachers were just as fascinated by Starstriker as Danny and the rest of the school, and when Mr Coker suggested that the bike and Danny should give a proper demonstration of their talents, everybody was delighted.

On the way home Starstriker remarked, 'I can see why you go to school everyday, Danny. All that equipment in the hall was marvellous. I can't wait to try it out again.' Danny had a hard job persuading Starstriker that school wasn't meant to be quite like it had been on the BMX's first visit.

6

Scram!

As more and more people got to hear about Danny and Starstriker there were endless knocks at the door and phone calls. The newspapers took up the story of the extraordinary bike. Photographers came down and almost blinded the Taggarts with their popping flashbulbs. For the first time in months, Sandra stopped torturing her hair with curlers all the time, and Mum even managed to persuade her to use a bit less lipstick.

'You can't be photographed like that,' said Mrs Taggart, one morning. 'Get that tomato sauce off your face.' Danny spluttered to himself and Sandra took the hint.

One afternoon a TV crew came along to film Danny and the BMX for the evening news. Mr and Mrs Taggart put on their best clothes and Sandra wore enough jingly bracelets for a hoopla stall.

That same evening the family sat glued to the television during the News, waiting to see themselves. When they did appear it was hilarious. There was Mrs Taggart scratching her ear, and Sandra fluttering her eyelashes like some desperate butterfly. Danny had a ridiculous grin on his face all the time, as if he'd just discovered the bath was full of green jelly.

‘I never thought we’d get on telly,’ laughed Mrs Taggart, and at that moment the telephone rang.

‘Shut the door, Mum,’ cried Sandra, as Mrs Taggart went to the phone. ‘It’s Top of the Pops’ on next and The Scram are going to be in it. They’re number six in the charts, and going up.’

Loud music leaped from the TV. A whirling group of youths burst onto the screen. They wore strange clothes and had multi-coloured hair that stuck out in every direction. The singer had an arrow stuck through his head.

Sandra moved her chair closer and she bounced up and down in time to the heavy beat. ‘Oh’, she murmured. ‘They’re beautiful.’

Mr Taggart watched for a moment. ‘What are they? Aliens?’

‘No! That’s The Scram. They’re the best group in the galaxy.’

‘Why has that one got an arrow through his head? If it’s a new cure for headaches I can understand him sticking it in his head, what with all that row they’re making.’

'Dad! Shut up! They're brill!' cried Sandra.

Danny watched 'Top of the Pops' through with his sister. He enjoyed it too, although he wasn't as impressed with The Scram as Sandra was. After that it was time for bed. It had been a tiring day.

The next morning there was a knock at the door and Mr Taggart opened it, expecting another cameraman or reporter. Instead he saw a large white Rolls Royce parked outside, and on the doorstep was someone extraordinary. He was short and dumpy and appeared to be drowning in a vast white fur coat. He wore extremely dark sunglasses and had a wine bottle in one hand and a half-empty glass in the other.

'Good evening,' he started, wobbling a bit.

'It's the morning,' Mr Taggart pointed out. The man stepped back in surprise and glanced at the sky.

'Great Aunt Winifred! So it is!' He waved his bottle majestically in the air and said, 'That's the sun up there you know. See? That little shiny thing.'

Mr Taggart waited patiently. 'Is there anything I can do for you?' The man staggered forward and pulled his sun glasses down over his nose to look at Mr Taggart more easily.

'Yes there is,' he cried. 'Oh yes,yes, yes! I am – I am – hic!' he burped, slopping more wine into his glass. 'I am – I've forgotten. Hic!'

Mr Taggart began to close the door, thoroughly fed up. The little man lurched forward. 'No, no, don't leave me. I'll be good. I say, did you know your face goes round and round and round? How extraordinary. It does you know – round and round. Anyhow, I was saying, who am I? My name is Stiff Pilchard.'

'Stiff What?'

'No, no, no, no. Not Stiff What. That's not right at all. Stiff Pilchard – but you can call me Stiff.'

'Oh,' nodded Mr Taggart.

'And I am hic! Pardon. I am the manager of The Scram. Have you heard of them? They play things you know, guitars and drums, bang bang, twang twang. They make records, you know.'

Mr Taggart was gradually making sense of Stiff Pilchard's drunken chatter. 'Ah yes – they were on TV last night. One of them had an arrow through his head.'

'Probably, probably,' said Stiff Pilchard. 'He had an axe stuck in it last week. But listen, my dear, dear friend. Hic!' Here Stiff leaned against Mr Taggart and draped one furry arm round his shoulders. 'We want you to make a video film for our new number. It's called 'Riding High' and when we saw Danny and Sharkbiter last night, we thought *Fantastic*! We'll ask Danny and his family to be in our video, hic! I say, would you like a drink?'

Mr Taggart unwrapped himself from the furry arm and asked Stiff to come inside. After Mrs Taggart had taken away his wine bottle and made him drink a lot of black coffee, Stiff slowly returned to a reasonable state.He went over the idea for the video again and said there would be quite a big fee to be paid to Danny and his family for their part in the film – if they wished to do it.

Sandra had been listening in, her eyes as wide as her mouth. 'Of course we'll do it!' She clung to Mum's arm and danced round her. 'Oh great! Making a video with Scram. Actually working with *them*! Help, I'd better go and wash my hair!' And she vanished upstairs.

'She seems quite keen on the idea,' smiled Mum. Since Danny and Dad also agreed, the whole thing was settled, and Stiff went rolling back to his Rolls Royce, promising he would be back in a couple of days, ready to film in the park.

Sure enough, two days later a large truck squeaked to a stop outside the Taggart's home. When the rear door was rolled up Danny discovered it was full of people – not to mention drum kits, guitars, amplifiers, stands and a hundred bits and pieces. The Scram were lounging about on a couple of ancient settees. 'We always travel like this,' said one, introducing himself as Derek. 'We get mobbed by our fans otherwise, so we hide away in this old truck. Good, isn't it? That's Mickey – Nutter – Bill.'

Each member stood up and bowed, then they all fell over as the truck set off with a jolt. By the time they reached the park, the Taggarts were firm friends with The Scram. Mr Taggart even tried on Nutter's arrow.

At the park the truck was unloaded and Stiff outlined the filming plan. 'Group, you set up in the children's play area. I want a camera on top of the slide, and another working from the swing for some fancy moving shots.'

'What do I do?' asked Danny. Stiff waved his furry arms about. 'I want you to zip around the play stuff okay? You know, a bit fancy. At the end you come charging across the park and do a leap over The Scram, okay? Great stuff! Right, everybody move!'

Starstriker, who had been very quiet up till now, rolled gently back and forth beside Danny. 'Is that man all right? Why does he wear a coat that's five sizes too large for him?'

'I don't know,' answered Danny. 'Come on, Scram's started.'

There was a thunder of drums from Scram and three guitars at full volume blasted the air. Nutter, with the arrow back in his head, began leaping around, swinging his mike round his head like a lassoo. Suddenly he snatched at it and sang.

'Yah! When I see my baby, I'm really riding high . . .'

Danny zoomed into view, twisting round the play equipment and performing jerky jumps and long wheelies. 'Great!' yelled Stiff. 'A dancing bicycle! Everybody join in!'

Mum and Dad and Sandra started to jerk about, waving their arms and legs madly. 'It's not like the old days, is it?' puffed Mrs Taggart.

'Come on Mum,' cried Sandra. 'Copy me!'

'If I dance like that I'll end up in knots,' Mum panted.

'Dance on the see-saw!' ordered Stiff, and Sandra danced her way up and down the see-saw. She was pretty good. Then Stiff told Mum and Dad to climb onto the roundabout and wriggle and twist up there.

Suddenly there was a terrible bellow and Creakyboots, the park-keeper appeared, charging across the grass on his mended racing bike. 'Oi! What do you think you're doing? Turn that radio off! No bikes in the park. Get those adults off the play equipment – that's not allowed either. Go on, scram!'

Nobody took any notice. The film's climax was fast approaching. Danny and Starstriker were lined up for their jump, the Taggarts were dancing themselves giddy and Scram were going absolutely bananas, yelling and screaming and smashing their instruments in wild abandon.

'Yah! I'm riding high, riding high!' screeched Nutter. From one side Creakyboots whizzed into the playground, and from the other Danny and Starbiker powered into their final leap.

'Danny!' cried Starstriker. 'There's a bike in the way – we're heading for a wipe-out!' There was an ear-shattering smash as the BMX, trying to avoid the park-keeper, came down smack in the middle of The Scram. The group hurled themselves out of the way, guitars flying off at odd angles, the drum kit collapsing in a thunderous heap, and the amplifiers going up in belching smoke, whining and squealing and making terrible bass noises which sounded more like hippos with toothache than anything else.

The din died away. Scram staggered about in the smoke and ruins. The Taggarts had frozen in horror. Danny stood astride Starstriker, amazed that they were still upright amongst the wreckage. Creakyboots was still wildly waving his arms about.

'I said no cycling and no adults on the play equipment and no radios!' he shouted.

Danny swallowed, wondering what would happen next. The Taggarts rather sheepishly climbed down from the roundabout. They all looked for Stiff Pilchard. He was dancing all by himself, round and round in little circles.

'It was great! he said. 'What a video! Incredible! What a wow!' Stiff rushed over to Creakyboots and pumped his hand. 'You were amazing! What a finish! It will look terrific!'

Creakyboots scratched his head. 'Who are you?' he demanded. Stiff explained everything and Creakyboots began to smile. 'Really? So this is The Scram is it? That's my favourite group. Could I have your autographs?'

So the disastrous end wasn't a disaster at all. Stiff and The Scram went away delighted. Creakyboots went home happy, and the Taggarts went home tired, but well paid. Sandra was in seventh heaven, all dreamy eyed.

'Nutter kissed my hand,' she murmured.

'Take care it doesn't fall off,' muttered Starstriker.

7

A thief in the night

As the days went by, Danny's fame spread. He carried on as before, dashing about on his BMX and enjoying himself. Sandra got a bit upset though. She spent so much time tidying her hair and putting on make-up and making sure she looked like a beauty queen – and what for? Everybody ignored her and took snapshots of her ugly brother instead. It was most unfair. She didn't cheer up until she received a signed photograph of all The Scram through the post.

'Look!' she cried. 'They've all signed their names, and Nutter's even put a kiss beside his.'

'No wonder they call him Nutter,' smirked Danny. Mrs Taggart gave him a playful tap.

'I think it's very nice,' she said, and glanced over her daughter's shoulders at the photograph. 'Goodness! Is that an axe stuck in his head?'

Sandra sighed deeply. 'Mmmmmm. Doesn't he look wonderful?' Before Danny could make any smart replies Mr Taggart came in with the rest of the morning post.

'Do you know what this is?'

'Don't tell me The Scram have sent you a photo too?' laughed Mum. 'Got any kisses from Nutter?'

Dad ignored her. 'It's a cheque,' he said. 'And it's quite a large one. That song of The Scram's, Riding High, is doing very well in the charts and we get some of the money they make because we were in the video for it. The great thing is that there will probably be several more cheques like this one.'

'Yippee!' yelled Danny. 'We could get a Rolls Royce.'

Dad shook his head. 'No, I don't think so. We shall have to think very carefully about what to do with it.' And he tucked the cheque into his jacket pocket and went out to have a think.

Meanwhile, other people were also planning things to do with the Taggart family. A lot of people had read the papers and discovered all about Starstriker, and one reader had the bright idea that if he could get hold of the marvellous BMX he would be able to make a great deal of money. A bike like that, thought Charlie Slark, must be worth a fortune.

Nobody in the Taggart family noticed the short, thin, dark-haired man wandering up and down their road. Charlie sauntered about for an hour or two, watching the house and noticing everything. He counted the number of people in the house and looked at the windows. Charlie smiled to himself. This job was going to be as easy as pie.

That same night, about three o'clock, Charlie crept into the Taggart's front garden. He went to the front door and listened through the letter-box for a while. Then he walked across the flowerbed to the window. From his jacket he pulled out a bunch of thin tools. He wiggled one round the edge of the window frame and a moment later the window sprang open and Charlie stepped into the dark front room.

Upstairs Mr Taggart was snoring like an old motorbike and Mrs Taggart had her head buried beneath two pillows. She always slept like that, otherwise she was deafened by the bike revving up right next to her.

Downstairs, Charlie tiptoed into the hall and saw the dim shape of Starstriker leaning quietly by the wall near the front door. Charlie grinned in the darkness and edged forward, his practised feet as quiet as a pair of dead rats.

'Danny!' The helmet by Danny's bed sparkled in the gloom.

'Danny, I think you should know something. Wakey, wakey,' said Starstriker gently.

Danny stirred and turned towards the helmet. 'That's better. Come on Danny. Somebody is trying to steal me. Wake up.' Danny opened his eyes and looked at the little shining stars. 'Ah', murmured Starstriker. 'Awake at last. Danny, I'm being stolen. There's a nasty little man down here with a moustache and he's trying to open the front door and take me out.'

Danny jerked upright and switched on his light. 'Don't let him Starstriker! Don't let him!'

'Oh, you want me to stop him, do you? I thought you'd be dashing to my aid. Well there's bravery for you. I get woken up in the middle of the night and I have to do all the dirty work as well.'

'Stop him!' pleaded Danny.

'Will you get me some mag wheels if I stop him?'

'I'll try, I'll try, but they're very expensive. Please Starstriker!'

'Well if I can't have mag wheels will you get me those nice reflectors that go on my wheel spokes?'

'Yes, yes, yes, yes!' Danny bounced up and down on his bed, hardly able to control his impatience.

'Oh well,' murmured Starstriker. That will do. Here goes.'

The helmet stopped twinkling. Danny crept to his door and opened it a fraction. Strange noises came from below. Charlie had managed to open the front door and was now wheeling the BMX out into the night. Suddenly the bike reversed back into the house at high speed, right out of Charlie's hands. The thief looked back in astonishment. Then Starstriker came hurtling forward and prodded Charlie hard in the backside.

'Hey! Geroff! Oi! Stop it! Ow! Pack it in! I'll get you!'

Charlie turned on Starstriker and seized the handlebars. He threw his legs over the frame and forced himself firmly onto the saddle. 'Now we'll see who's boss around here,' he snarled, and started to pedal down the garden path. Just as they reached the front gate, Starstriker came to a halt and began a crazy, high-speed spin, pirouetting round on the back wheel, while Charlie clung on for dear life and let out a terrified wail.

'Woooooaaahhhhhhhoooooooooeeeeeeeeeek!'

When Starstriker stopped spinning, Charlie's eyeballs were going round in his head like ball-bearings, but he was still sitting firmly on the saddle. The BMX began to buck and leap like a young wild horse, charging up and down the path, dancing from side to side and throwing Charlie up in the air so that his legs waved about like sails on a windmill and his hat tipped down over his face.

At last he could stand it no longer and with an anxious squeak he let go of the handlebars and was thrown out into the silent road. Starstriker zipped back into the house and slammed the door shut with his front wheel.

The noise had woken the whole family and they had watched Starstriker's circus show from the safety of the front room. They were still laughing after Charlie had disappeared at full speed down the street.

Mum discovered the open window and closed it once more. Then she saw their dog, Snapper, lying fast asleep in one of the armchairs. 'Take a look at that,' she said. 'What a guard-dog! It's a good thing we've got Starstriker. I reckon he's a guard-bike. You did a good job there, Starstriker.'

All the bike's little stars went off like fireworks. 'Thank you very much', said Starstriker, his voice bursting with pride. 'Did you hear that Danny? I'm a guard-bike. I did a good job.'

'Big-head,' grunted Danny, and went back upstairs to bed.

But Charlie Slark had not given up hope. He knew that the BMX could make him a lot of money and he was determined to get hold of Starstriker by one means or another. He decided that what he needed was a little help, or to be more exact, he needed some big help and Charlie knew that the best big help came in the shape of Fats Donovan.

Fats Donovan had once been a boxer and he liked to think that he was still as tough and strong as he had been when he was younger. Fats Donovan could lift two people at the same time, one under each arm. He could crack brazil nuts simply by squeezing them in one hand. And Fats Donovan was always ready to take on a challenge.

He was still rather taken aback though when Charlie told him what he needed Fats for, and Fats laughed with a roar like a train bursting from a tunnel.

'Can't you steal a boy's bike any more, Charlie!' And he slapped Charlie on the back so hard that Charlie's false teeth popped out. 'Of course I can, but it's not an ordinary bike. It's Starstriker.'

Fats Donovan nodded his big bald head. 'Oh yes. I've read about that bike. Well what's the plan then?'

'We're going to hijack it. We're going to come up alongside on my motorbike and you're going to grab the bike.'

'What about the boy?' asked Fats.

'Knock him off,' snapped Charlie. Fats Donovan grinned, and Charlie laid a warning hand on the boxer's arm. 'Don't be fooled. That bike's tough.'

Fats allowed a slow smile to spread across his face and he flexed his muscles. 'So am I!'

The very next day Danny was riding Starstriker down the road, enjoying the feel of the sun on his back, when he became aware of a spluttering roar behind, getting louder and louder. He glanced back and saw the fast-approaching motorbike but couldn't recognise the riders and thought nothing of it. The next moment the motorbike was alongside and Charlie grinned across evilly. Behind Charlie sat Fats Donovan, and he started to reach out with an arm that was thicker than a lampost and had a hand on the end of it like the grabber of a JCB.

'Hey hey!' roared Fats. 'Get a bit closer Charlie and we'll soon have it!'

'That's a remarkably smelly motorbike next to us, Danny,' said Starstriker. 'Shall we find some fresh air?'

'Good idea,' smiled Danny. Starstriker speeded up and the motorbike fell back for a few seconds.

'After them!' screeched Fats. 'Get them!' Charlie twisted the accelerator and they shot after the shining BMX and drew alongside again. Starstriker put on another spurt of speed.

'What are they playing at?' yelled Charlie, chasing after them once more and coming alongside, but only for a second, for the BMX shot forwards up the road.

By now both bikes were steaming along at a fine speed. Charlie revved up to top speed and closed in for the kill. 'This time we've got them,' cried Fats. 'Hallo!' he leered at Danny.

'Bye bye,' chorused Danny and Starstriker and they zoomed away and vanished, leaving the motorbike pelting along at top speed. A siren shrieked through the air and a police car raced up to Charlie and Fats, forcing them to slow down and stop. The last thing Danny saw was two policeman booking the pair for speeding.

'Fancy trying to overtake me,' murmured Starstriker. 'I wonder what they wanted.'

'Probably my autograph,' said Danny, with a hidden smile.

Starstriker coughed politely. 'Now who's a big-head?' he asked.

8

Starbiker!

Mr Taggart sat at the breakfast table looking very thoughtful. 'What's the matter with you,' asked Mum, busily scraping the charcoal off the toast Sandra had just burnt.

Dad glanced round the table at the rest of the family. 'I've been wondering what to do with the money from the video and I thought maybe I could start up a little business – a shop maybe. I've been out of work for over a year and there's no chance of me finding a job any other way. What do you think?'

Mum was impressed. 'Sounds very sensible to me.' Danny wasn't so sure. He had set his heart on a Rolls Royce. A shop didn't sound very exciting at all. But Sandra's eyes lit up and she clapped her hands.

'You could start a hairdressing salon!'

'You know, Danny,' said Starstriker quietly, 'I'm so glad I haven't got any hair – the amount of time people spend washing and curling and drying.'

'Listen bike,' snapped Danny, 'I spend as much time washing and polishing you as Sandra does on her hair. What's the difference?'

'I'm beautiful,' Starstriker pointed out.

'Oh thanks a lot!' huffed Sandra. 'I shall be beautiful one day. You're just a big-head, sparkle-bonce.'

'Pimple face,' snorted Starstriker.

'Big-head, big-saddle, big-tyres, big ... big-galop!' Sandra spluttered.

'All right, all right, 'Mum said soothingly. 'I think Dad was going to say something more.'

Mr Taggart leaned back in his chair. 'What do you think about me starting up a bike shop, selling BMXs and the like?'

'Brilliant!' cried Danny.

Starstriker glittered. 'I think it's a very good suggestion. Of course, you don't know very much about bicycles but I shall be able to help you.' Mrs Taggart said she thought there already was a cycle shop in the High Street.

'Yes I know, but it's not a very good one. Mine would be different. I saw a shop for sale in the High Street yesterday. With the money coming from the video I think we could afford to start up there.'

Things went ahead as planned. The days seemed to fly past. The little shop needed cleaning, then painting. The showcases arrived and best of all, a truckload of bikes, mostly BMXs and racers. The place looked marvellous. Mr Taggart was so proud that Mum said he would burst all his shirt buttons if he puffed out his chest any further.

A big sign went up with the name of the shop – RIDING HIGH.

'We ought to get somebody famous to open the shop, like the TV star at the supermarket,' suggested Danny.

'Why don't we ask The Scram?' said Sandra.

'Do you think they would?' asked Dad. 'They're very famous.'

Sandra smoothed back her hair and closed her eyes. 'They'll do anything for me,' she claimed, and she was right too. The Scram said they would be delighted to open the new shop. They arranged to arrive on a flat lorry, and play their way down the High Street, until they reached the shop.

Mr Taggart had put adverts all over the place about The Scram opening the new bike shop. He hoped a lot of people would turn up but even he was amazed by the huge crowd that gathered outside RIDING HIGH on the grand opening day. All the BMXers from far and wide came along, riding up and down the pavements and generally getting in everybody's way.

All at once the crowd screamed. 'They're coming! They're coming!' Young girls began to yell and tear their hair as The Scram appeared, slowly making their way down the High Street. The heavy beat of their hit song thundered through the air.

The truck came to a halt and the group waved to their cheering fans. Then they launched into

'Riding High' all over again. The music blasted out and the street filled with twirling, dancing people of all ages. The Scram obviously thought this was great because they turned up the volume even louder.

A large truck carrying sheets of glass crept along, trying to get through the seething crowd, but just as it drew level with the pop group every pane of glass shattered from the hammering noise. Slivers of glass cascaded onto the road and there followed a series of loud bangs as following cars had all their tyres punctured. Horns blared. Brakes squealed. Angry drivers flung open their doors and marched up and down waving their fists in the air and looking very grim.

The Scram became silent, watching the results of their loud playing with awkward horror. One by one they slipped off the platform and crept into the shop. Nutter, who this time was wearing a large foam saw on his head, looked at Mr Taggart and said, 'I think we've got a problem.'

'I think you have,' said Mr Taggart, looking at the waving saw.

A plume of smoke began to twist up into the sky and a scream broke from the crowd. Drivers were now running to the sides of the street and frantic mothers grabbed their children and retreated to the safety of the shops. Mrs Taggart climbed onto the truck and stared over the still and silent cars.

'There's a blaze started in one of the cars,' she said. 'I hope they put it out quickly. That car's right next to a petrol tanker.'

'Oh no! If that goes up it will blow the whole High Street to little pieces. It's a bomb on four wheels!' said Mr Taggart.

They stared white-faced at the leaping flames. A siren sounded and a fire engine hurtled down the street, only to come to a screeching halt, its path blocked by the mass of cars and vans that were lying punctured and unmoveable. It was impossible to get through. 'They'll never do it,' murmured Mr Taggart. 'There's going to be an almighty explosion.'

Danny felt a nudge in his back. It was Starstriker. 'Time to go,' said the BMX quietly. Danny gulped.

'What can we do?'

'I don't know yet. Just get on and let's go.' Danny pulled on the twinkling helmet and skidded out of the shop.

'Get to the fire-engine,' said Danny. The BMX angled up for a jump.

'Full powerboost,' Starstriker said calmly.

'You bet!' grinned Danny. The bike accelerated like lightning and hurtled towards the pile of cars, then ZAMMMMMM!! Starstriker shot into the air, arching through the black smoke and landing with a screech beside the fire-engine. The bike slewed to a halt.

'Phew,' muttered Danny.

'You didn't say Yeeehah!' Starstriker pointed out.

'I forgot. Come on. Let's get moving before it's too late.'

Danny explained rapidly to the Fire Chief what they had in mind, and although the Fire Chief wasn't happy about the idea there wasn't much choice. The firemen unrolled a hose and Danny fixed one end to Starstriker. The BMX glittered.

'Can we jump up there?'

'I don't think so,' said Danny. 'There's too much smoke and I can't see where to land. We can't get through the cars either. We shall have to hop.'

'Hop! I've never hopped anywhere before,' said Starstriker.

'Now's your chance then,' grinned Danny, climbing onto the saddle. 'You'll have to let me control the hops.'

The BMX shuddered. 'I knew I should have stayed quietly at home today. Okay, let's go!' Danny gripped the bars and headed for the tangle of cars ahead. The black smoke was now belching out and punching into the air like a giant fist. Danny pulled Starstriker up on the rear wheel and forced the bike up the back of a car and onto its roof. He stopped and glanced around. 'That way,' he ordered, twisting Starstriker in the right direction. The bike began to plunge from one car to the next, sometimes leaping from one roof to another, sometimes clattering across bonnets and boots.

Soon they were lost to view. They had vanished into the choking smoke and fumes. The crowd held their breath. All that could be seen was the grey snake of a hose, still writhing about as Starstriker and Danny moved closer and closer to the blaze.

Danny's eyes were streaming and his face and clothes were streaked with soot and bits of charred rubbish from the fire. Starstriker was almost black and his little stars shone dully through the grime. 'Where are we?' demanded the bike.

'Almost there,' coughed Danny, forcing the BMX from the roof of a car to the top of a taxi. 'It's that car there.'

They crashed down to road level and Danny grabbed the hose. He yelled as loudly as he could and a moment later water raced down the pipe and gushed from the nozzle. There was a tremendous hissing and horrible smell of hot, wet metal. The flames from the car leaped back and shrank from the deadly water. The tanker's tyres were already on fire and Danny soaked them just in time. The smoke began to drift away and Danny hosed down the sides of the steaming tanker to cool the blistered metal.

Danny closed his eyes and let out a long, long sigh of relief. He felt something push at his back. It was Starstriker. 'Are you going to leave me all black and smelly like this?' the BMX demanded. 'I stink.'

Danny laughed and turned the hose on the bike. 'Ohwowowoh! That's lovely,' twinkled Starstriker. 'There's nothing like a cold shower!' Bath-time was rudely interrupted by a surge of people rushing back onto the street. They crowded round Danny and his bike.

Stiff Pilchard grasped Danny's waist and danced round and round. 'Brilliant bravery!' he shouted. 'Such as I've never seen before. I know your bike's Starstriker, but I reckon you're a Starbiker!

'Three cheers for Starbiker!' yelled the crowd, carrying Danny shoulder high.

'I'm going to build you and your friends a proper BMX track and all,' promised Stiff. 'After what my group have done and your bravery, it's the least I can do.'

Danny's face just about split with a giant grin. 'Oh wow!' Stiff smiled back. 'Don't thank me. The Scram are going to pay for it out of their earnings.

Stupid twits!' But nobody heard the last remark because The Scram had started playing again and everybody was dancing and singing, especially Sandra, who was doing a duet with Nutter. She had an arrow stuck in her head, her eyes were shut and her hands clasped together in ecstasy. The arrow wobbled frantically, and she smiled up at Nutter. Starstriker gave a long sigh.

'Danny? Your sister is –' There was a long pause. Danny waited to find out what Sandra was. But the glittering bike just sighed again. 'Oh, never mind. It's terribly noisy round here,' Starstriker went on. 'Can't we go for a nice quiet ride somewhere . . . just an ordinary, slow, bike ride?'

Danny nodded. He felt the same way. There had been quite enough excitement for the time being. He climbed on to the saddle and pedalled away. Quite soon the noise and the people were out of sight and silence settled round them both. Starstriker didn't say a word, and Danny kept quiet too. It was nicer that way. The sun glinted on the bike's silver frame and together they went slowly and quietly on their own ordinary bike ride. Danny and Starstriker both knew that quiet rides like this were going to be very rare occasions. They were going to enjoy being ordinary while they could . . . until the next extra-ordinary adventure came their way.